50 Israeli Breakfast Spreads Recipes for Home

By: Kelly Johnson

Table of Contents

- Shakshuka
- Hummus with tahini
- Labneh with olive oil and za'atar
- Israeli salad
- Sabich sandwich
- Bureka with cheese filling
- Malawach with grated tomato
- Fava bean stew
- Jerusalem bagel with sesame seeds
- Turkish-style scrambled eggs with vegetables (Menemen)
- Moroccan-style sardines in tomato sauce
- Bourekas with potato filling
- Challah French toast with date syrup
- Yemenite soup (Marak Temani)
- Grilled eggplant with tahini sauce
- Roasted red pepper spread (Muhammara)
- Grilled halloumi cheese
- Bulgarian-style cheese pastries (Börek)
- Sweet potato pancakes
- Matbucha (Tomato and roasted pepper salad)
- Israeli cheese platter with olives and nuts
- Iraqi-style stuffed vegetables (Dolma)
- Moroccan-style mint tea
- Za'atar bread
- Tunisian-style spicy carrot salad (Salata Meshwiya)
- Turkish coffee
- Armenian cucumber yogurt salad (Jajik)
- Tunisian-style fried egg with spicy tomato sauce (Ojja)
- Iraqi-style date cookies (Kleicha)
- Cheese borek with filo pastry
- Yemenite bread (Jachnun) with grated tomato
- Turkish-style stuffed peppers (Biber Dolması)
- Moroccan-style semolina pancakes (Baghrir)
- Georgian cheese bread (Khachapuri)
- Date and walnut bread

- Bulgarian-style yogurt with honey and nuts
- Turkish-style spinach and feta borek
- Moroccan-style orange and almond salad
- Iraqi-style kubba (Stuffed bulgur wheat dumplings)
- Armenian-style apricot compote
- Georgian-style walnut and red pepper dip (Adjika)
- Iraqi-style beef kebabs (Kebab Hindi)
- Turkish-style simit bread with sesame seeds
- Moroccan-style spiced olives
- Egyptian-style ful medames
- Armenian-style cheese burek
- Turkish-style spinach and feta omelette
- Moroccan-style honey and almond pastries (M'hanncha)
- Turkish-style fried eggplant with yogurt and garlic (Ali Nazik)
- Armenian-style tahini cake

Shakshuka

Ingredients:

- 2 tablespoons olive oil
- 1 onion, diced
- 2 cloves garlic, minced
- 1 bell pepper, diced
- 4 cups tomatoes, diced (or canned diced tomatoes)
- 1 teaspoon ground cumin
- 1 teaspoon smoked paprika
- 1/2 teaspoon chili powder (adjust to taste)
- Salt and pepper to taste
- 4-6 eggs
- Fresh parsley or cilantro, chopped (for garnish)
- Crumbled feta cheese (optional, for serving)
- Crusty bread or pita, for serving

Instructions:

Heat olive oil in a large skillet over medium heat. Add diced onion and cook until softened, about 5 minutes.
Add minced garlic and diced bell pepper to the skillet, and cook for another 2-3 minutes until fragrant.
Stir in diced tomatoes, ground cumin, smoked paprika, chili powder, salt, and pepper. Simmer the mixture for about 10-15 minutes until the sauce has thickened slightly.
Using a spoon, create small wells in the sauce and crack the eggs into each well.
Cover the skillet and cook for 5-7 minutes, or until the egg whites are set but the yolks are still runny (cook longer if you prefer firmer yolks).
Once the eggs are cooked to your liking, remove the skillet from heat. Garnish with chopped parsley or cilantro and crumbled feta cheese, if desired.
Serve the Shakshuka hot directly from the skillet, with crusty bread or pita on the side for dipping.

Enjoy your flavorful and comforting Shakshuka breakfast!

Hummus with tahini

Ingredients:

- 1 can (15 ounces) chickpeas (garbanzo beans), drained and rinsed
- 1/4 cup tahini (sesame paste)
- 2-3 tablespoons freshly squeezed lemon juice
- 1-2 cloves garlic, minced (adjust to taste)
- 2-4 tablespoons extra virgin olive oil
- 1/2 teaspoon ground cumin
- Salt, to taste
- Water, as needed

Optional toppings:

- Drizzle of olive oil
- Sprinkle of paprika or sumac
- Chopped fresh parsley or cilantro
- Toasted pine nuts or sesame seeds

Instructions:

In a food processor, combine the drained chickpeas, tahini, lemon juice, minced garlic, olive oil, ground cumin, and a pinch of salt.
Process the mixture until smooth and creamy, scraping down the sides of the food processor as needed. If the hummus is too thick, you can add a tablespoon or two of water to achieve your desired consistency.
Taste the hummus and adjust the seasoning by adding more lemon juice, garlic, or salt as needed.
Once the hummus reaches the desired consistency and flavor, transfer it to a serving bowl.
Drizzle some extra virgin olive oil over the top of the hummus and sprinkle with paprika or sumac for added flavor and color.
Garnish with chopped fresh parsley or cilantro, and toasted pine nuts or sesame seeds if desired.
Serve the hummus with tahini as a dip with pita bread, crackers, or fresh vegetable sticks.

Enjoy your homemade hummus with tahini, a delicious and nutritious snack or appetizer!

Labneh with olive oil and za'atar

Ingredients:

- 2 cups plain yogurt (preferably full-fat)
- 1/2 teaspoon salt
- Olive oil, for drizzling
- Za'atar spice blend, for sprinkling

Instructions:

Place a fine mesh strainer over a bowl and line it with cheesecloth or a clean kitchen towel.
Stir the salt into the plain yogurt.
Pour the yogurt into the lined strainer. Gather the edges of the cheesecloth or towel and tie them together to form a bundle.
Place the bundle in the refrigerator and let the yogurt strain for 12 to 24 hours. The longer you strain it, the thicker the labneh will become.
Once strained to your desired thickness, remove the labneh from the cheesecloth or towel and transfer it to a serving bowl.
Drizzle olive oil over the top of the labneh.
Sprinkle za'atar spice blend generously over the olive oil.
Serve the labneh with olive oil and za'atar as a spread for bread, crackers, or vegetables. It's also delicious as a topping for salads or grilled meats.

Enjoy the creamy texture and flavorful combination of labneh with olive oil and za'atar!

Israeli salad

Ingredients:

- 2 large tomatoes, diced
- 1 cucumber, diced
- 1 bell pepper (red, yellow, or green), diced
- 1/2 red onion, finely chopped
- 2 tablespoons fresh parsley, finely chopped
- 2 tablespoons fresh mint, finely chopped (optional)
- Juice of 1-2 lemons, to taste
- 2-3 tablespoons extra virgin olive oil
- Salt and pepper, to taste

Instructions:

In a large mixing bowl, combine the diced tomatoes, cucumber, bell pepper, red onion, parsley, and mint (if using).
Drizzle the olive oil over the vegetables.
Squeeze the lemon juice over the salad, starting with the juice of one lemon and adjusting to taste. Be careful not to make the salad too acidic; you can always add more lemon juice later if needed.
Season the salad with salt and pepper, to taste.
Toss the salad gently to combine all the ingredients and evenly distribute the dressing.
Taste and adjust the seasoning as needed, adding more salt, pepper, or lemon juice if desired.
Let the salad sit for a few minutes to allow the flavors to meld together before serving.
Serve the Israeli salad as a side dish or accompaniment to grilled meats, falafel, or other Middle Eastern dishes.

Enjoy the refreshing and vibrant flavors of Israeli salad!

Sabich sandwich

Ingredients:

For the filling:

- 4 pita bread rounds
- 2 large or 4 small eggs, hard-boiled and sliced
- 2 medium potatoes, peeled and sliced into thin rounds
- 1 medium eggplant, sliced into thin rounds
- 1/4 cup vegetable oil (for frying)
- Salt, to taste
- Ground black pepper, to taste
- Tahini sauce (store-bought or homemade)
- Amba sauce (pickled mango sauce, optional)
- Chopped fresh parsley or cilantro, for garnish

For serving (optional):

- Pickled cucumbers
- Pickled turnips
- Hot sauce or harissa

Instructions:

Heat vegetable oil in a large skillet over medium heat.
Fry the potato slices in batches until golden brown and crispy. Remove them from the skillet and drain excess oil on paper towels. Season with salt and pepper to taste.
In the same skillet, fry the eggplant slices until golden brown and tender. Remove them from the skillet and drain excess oil on paper towels. Season with salt and pepper to taste.
Warm the pita bread rounds in the oven or on a skillet until soft and pliable.
To assemble each Sabich sandwich, open a pita bread round and spread a generous amount of tahini sauce inside.
Layer the sliced hard-boiled eggs, fried potato slices, and fried eggplant slices inside the pita bread.
Drizzle with additional tahini sauce and amba sauce (if using).
Garnish with chopped fresh parsley or cilantro.
If desired, add pickled cucumbers, pickled turnips, and a drizzle of hot sauce or harissa.
Serve the Sabich sandwiches immediately, while warm.

Enjoy the delicious flavors and textures of Sabich sandwiches, a beloved Israeli street food!

Bureka with cheese filling

Ingredients:

For the dough:

- 2 cups all-purpose flour
- 1 teaspoon salt

- 1/2 cup unsalted butter, chilled and diced
- 1/2 cup cold water
- 1 egg, beaten (for egg wash)

For the cheese filling:

- 1 cup crumbled feta cheese
- 1 cup shredded mozzarella cheese
- 1/4 cup grated Parmesan cheese
- 1/4 cup chopped fresh parsley
- 1/4 teaspoon ground black pepper
- 1 egg, beaten (for binding)

Instructions:

In a large mixing bowl, combine the all-purpose flour and salt. Add the chilled diced butter to the flour mixture.
Use your fingertips or a pastry cutter to work the butter into the flour until the mixture resembles coarse crumbs.
Gradually add the cold water to the flour mixture, mixing until a dough forms. If the dough is too dry, add a little more water, 1 tablespoon at a time.
Turn the dough out onto a lightly floured surface and knead it gently until smooth.
Shape the dough into a ball, wrap it in plastic wrap, and refrigerate for at least 30 minutes.
Preheat the oven to 375°F (190°C). Line a baking sheet with parchment paper.
In a mixing bowl, combine the crumbled feta cheese, shredded mozzarella cheese, grated Parmesan cheese, chopped fresh parsley, and ground black pepper. Mix well.
On a lightly floured surface, roll out the chilled dough into a thin rectangle, about 1/8 inch thick.
Use a sharp knife or pizza cutter to cut the dough into smaller rectangles, each about 3x6 inches in size.
Place a spoonful of the cheese filling onto one half of each rectangle of dough, leaving a border around the edges.
Fold the other half of the dough over the filling to enclose it, forming a square or rectangle shape. Press the edges firmly to seal.
Use a fork to crimp the edges of the pastries to ensure they are sealed.
Place the filled pastries onto the prepared baking sheet. Brush the tops of the pastries with beaten egg wash.

Bake the Bureka in the preheated oven for 20-25 minutes, or until golden brown and crispy.
Remove the pastries from the oven and let them cool slightly before serving.
Serve the Bureka with cheese filling warm or at room temperature.

Enjoy the delicious and cheesy Bureka pastries as a snack or appetizer!

Malawach with grated tomato

Ingredients:

For the dough:

- 3 cups all-purpose flour
- 1 teaspoon salt
- 1 cup unsalted butter, melted
- 1 cup cold water

For the grated tomato topping:

- 2-3 ripe tomatoes, grated
- 2 cloves garlic, minced
- 2 tablespoons olive oil
- Salt and pepper to taste
- Optional toppings: chopped parsley, chopped green onions, or sliced olives

Instructions:

In a large mixing bowl, combine the all-purpose flour and salt. Gradually add the melted butter to the flour mixture, stirring until crumbly.

Slowly add the cold water to the mixture, kneading until a soft dough forms. You may need to adjust the amount of water slightly to achieve the right consistency.

Divide the dough into small balls, about the size of a golf ball. Cover the dough balls with a damp cloth and let them rest for about 30 minutes.

While the dough is resting, prepare the grated tomato topping. Grate the tomatoes using a box grater, discarding the skins. Place the grated tomatoes in a bowl and add minced garlic, olive oil, salt, and pepper. Mix well to combine.

After the dough has rested, take one dough ball and roll it out on a lightly floured surface into a thin circle or oval shape, about 1/8 inch thick.

Heat a non-stick skillet or griddle over medium heat. Once hot, place the rolled-out dough on the skillet and cook for 2-3 minutes on each side, or until golden brown and cooked through.

Repeat the rolling and cooking process with the remaining dough balls.

Once all the Malawach breads are cooked, serve them warm with the grated tomato topping spooned over the top.

Garnish the Malawach with chopped parsley, chopped green onions, or sliced olives if desired.

Serve the Malawach with grated tomato as a delicious and savory snack or appetizer.

Enjoy the flaky and flavorful Malawach with grated tomato!

Fava bean stew

Ingredients:

- 2 cups dried fava beans
- 4 cups water (for soaking)
- 2 tablespoons olive oil
- 1 onion, finely chopped
- 3 cloves garlic, minced
- 2 tomatoes, diced
- 1 teaspoon ground cumin
- 1 teaspoon ground coriander
- 1/2 teaspoon paprika
- Salt and pepper to taste

- Juice of 1 lemon
- Chopped fresh parsley or cilantro for garnish
- Optional toppings: hard-boiled eggs, sliced tomatoes, pickled vegetables

Instructions:

Rinse the dried fava beans under cold water and place them in a large bowl. Cover the beans with water and let them soak overnight or for at least 8 hours.

Drain the soaked fava beans and rinse them again under cold water. Place the beans in a large pot and cover them with fresh water. Bring the water to a boil over medium-high heat, then reduce the heat to low and simmer the beans for 45 minutes to 1 hour, or until they are tender. Skim off any foam that rises to the surface while cooking.

While the fava beans are cooking, heat olive oil in a skillet over medium heat. Add the chopped onion and cook until softened and translucent, about 5 minutes. Add the minced garlic and cook for an additional 1-2 minutes, until fragrant.

Add the diced tomatoes to the skillet with the onions and garlic. Cook for 5-7 minutes, stirring occasionally, until the tomatoes have softened and released their juices.

Once the fava beans are tender, drain them and transfer them to the skillet with the tomato mixture. Add ground cumin, ground coriander, paprika, salt, and pepper to taste. Stir to combine.

Cook the fava bean stew over medium-low heat for an additional 10-15 minutes, allowing the flavors to meld together.

Just before serving, squeeze the juice of one lemon over the stew and stir to incorporate.

Garnish the fava bean stew with chopped fresh parsley or cilantro.

Serve the fava bean stew hot, with optional toppings such as hard-boiled eggs, sliced tomatoes, or pickled vegetables.

Enjoy this hearty and flavorful fava bean stew as a comforting meal!

Jerusalem bagel with sesame seeds

Ingredients:

- 3 cups all-purpose flour
- 1 tablespoon granulated sugar
- 1 teaspoon salt
- 1 tablespoon instant yeast
- 1 cup warm water
- 2 tablespoons olive oil
- 1/4 cup sesame seeds

Instructions:

In a large mixing bowl, combine the all-purpose flour, sugar, salt, and instant yeast. Gradually add the warm water to the dry ingredients, stirring with a wooden spoon or dough hook attachment of a stand mixer, until a dough forms.

Knead the dough on a floured surface for about 5-7 minutes, or until it becomes smooth and elastic. Alternatively, you can use a stand mixer fitted with a dough hook to knead the dough.

Place the dough in a lightly greased bowl, cover it with a clean kitchen towel, and let it rise in a warm place for about 1 hour, or until doubled in size.

Preheat your oven to 400°F (200°C) and line a baking sheet with parchment paper.

Punch down the risen dough and divide it into 8 equal portions. Shape each portion into a long rope, about 8-10 inches in length.

Form each rope into a ring shape, overlapping the ends slightly, and press them together to seal.

Place the shaped bagels on the prepared baking sheet, leaving some space between each one.

Brush the tops of the bagels with olive oil and sprinkle sesame seeds over the top, pressing lightly to adhere.

Bake the Jerusalem bagels in the preheated oven for 15-20 minutes, or until they are golden brown and cooked through.

Remove the bagels from the oven and let them cool slightly on a wire rack before serving.

Serve the Jerusalem bagels warm or at room temperature. They can be enjoyed plain or with your favorite spreads, dips, or fillings.

Enjoy these delicious Jerusalem bagels with sesame seeds as a snack or accompaniment to your favorite dishes!

Turkish-style scrambled eggs with vegetables (Menemen)

Ingredients:

- 4 large eggs
- 2 tablespoons olive oil
- 1 onion, finely chopped
- 2 bell peppers (red, green, or yellow), diced
- 2 medium tomatoes, diced
- 2 cloves garlic, minced
- 1 teaspoon paprika
- 1/2 teaspoon ground cumin
- Salt and pepper to taste
- Fresh parsley or cilantro, chopped (for garnish)
- Crumbled feta cheese (optional, for serving)
- Crusty bread or pita, for serving

Instructions:

Heat the olive oil in a large skillet over medium heat.

Add the chopped onion to the skillet and cook until softened and translucent, about 5 minutes.

Add the diced bell peppers to the skillet and cook for another 3-4 minutes, until they start to soften.

Stir in the minced garlic and cook for 1 minute, until fragrant.

Add the diced tomatoes to the skillet and cook for 5-7 minutes, until they start to break down and release their juices.

Sprinkle the paprika, ground cumin, salt, and pepper over the vegetables, and stir to combine.

Crack the eggs directly into the skillet over the vegetable mixture. Use a spatula to gently scramble the eggs and incorporate them into the vegetables. Cook until the eggs are set but still slightly runny.

Once the eggs are cooked to your liking, remove the skillet from heat.

Sprinkle chopped fresh parsley or cilantro over the top of the Menemen.

Serve the Menemen hot, directly from the skillet, with crusty bread or pita on the side for dipping.

If desired, sprinkle crumbled feta cheese over the top of the Menemen before serving.

Enjoy the flavorful and comforting Turkish-style scrambled eggs with vegetables (Menemen) for breakfast or brunch!

Moroccan-style sardines in tomato sauce

Ingredients:

- 8 fresh sardines, cleaned and gutted
- 2 tablespoons olive oil
- 1 onion, finely chopped
- 2 cloves garlic, minced
- 2 tomatoes, diced
- 1 tablespoon tomato paste
- 1 teaspoon paprika
- 1/2 teaspoon ground cumin
- 1/2 teaspoon ground coriander
- 1/4 teaspoon ground cinnamon
- Pinch of cayenne pepper (optional, for heat)
- Salt and pepper to taste
- Fresh parsley or cilantro, chopped (for garnish)
- Lemon wedges, for serving

Instructions:

Heat the olive oil in a large skillet or saucepan over medium heat.
Add the chopped onion to the skillet and cook until softened and translucent, about 5 minutes.
Stir in the minced garlic and cook for another minute, until fragrant.
Add the diced tomatoes and tomato paste to the skillet, and cook for 5-7 minutes, until the tomatoes start to break down and form a sauce.
Stir in the paprika, ground cumin, ground coriander, ground cinnamon, cayenne pepper (if using), salt, and pepper. Mix well to combine the spices with the tomato sauce.
Reduce the heat to low and simmer the tomato sauce for another 5-10 minutes, until it thickens slightly.
Season the cleaned and gutted sardines with salt and pepper.
Carefully place the seasoned sardines into the simmering tomato sauce, making sure they are submerged in the sauce.
Cover the skillet or saucepan and let the sardines cook in the sauce for about 10-15 minutes, or until they are cooked through and tender. Be careful not to overcook the sardines, as they can become dry.
Once the sardines are cooked, remove the skillet from heat.
Sprinkle chopped fresh parsley or cilantro over the top of the Moroccan-style sardines in tomato sauce.
Serve the sardines hot, directly from the skillet, with lemon wedges on the side for squeezing over the fish.

Enjoy the aromatic and flavorful Moroccan-style sardines in tomato sauce with crusty bread or couscous on the side!

Bourekas with potato filling

Ingredients:

For the dough:

- 2 sheets of frozen puff pastry, thawed according to package instructions
- Flour, for dusting

For the potato filling:

- 2 large potatoes, peeled and diced
- 1 onion, finely chopped
- 2 cloves garlic, minced
- 2 tablespoons olive oil
- 1/2 teaspoon ground cumin
- 1/2 teaspoon paprika
- Salt and pepper to taste
- Chopped fresh parsley or cilantro (optional, for garnish)

For assembly:

- 1 egg, beaten (for egg wash)
- Sesame seeds or poppy seeds (optional, for topping)

Instructions:

Preheat your oven to 375°F (190°C) and line a baking sheet with parchment paper.
To make the potato filling, boil the diced potatoes in salted water until tender, about 10-15 minutes. Drain and set aside.
In a skillet, heat olive oil over medium heat. Add the chopped onion and cook until softened and translucent, about 5 minutes. Add the minced garlic and cook for another minute.
Add the boiled diced potatoes to the skillet with the onions and garlic. Mash the potatoes slightly with a fork or potato masher, leaving some texture. Stir in the ground cumin, paprika, salt, and pepper to taste. Cook for a few minutes until the flavors are well combined. Remove from heat and let the filling cool slightly.
On a lightly floured surface, unfold the thawed puff pastry sheets. Roll out each sheet slightly to flatten it and create a larger surface area.
Cut each puff pastry sheet into squares or rectangles, depending on the size you prefer.
Place a spoonful of the potato filling onto one half of each pastry square or rectangle, leaving a border around the edges.
Fold the other half of the pastry over the filling to enclose it, forming a triangle or rectangle shape. Press the edges firmly to seal.
Use a fork to crimp the edges of the pastries to ensure they are sealed.
Place the filled pastries onto the prepared baking sheet.
Brush the tops of the pastries with beaten egg wash and sprinkle sesame seeds or poppy seeds over the top, if desired.
Bake the Bourekas in the preheated oven for 20-25 minutes, or until they are golden brown and puffed up.
Remove the pastries from the oven and let them cool slightly on a wire rack.
Garnish the Bourekas with chopped fresh parsley or cilantro, if desired.
Serve the Bourekas with potato filling warm or at room temperature.

Enjoy these delicious Bourekas with potato filling as a snack, appetizer, or part of a brunch spread!

Yemenite soup (Marak Temani)

Ingredients:

- 1 tablespoon vegetable oil
- 1 onion, finely chopped
- 2 cloves garlic, minced
- 2 carrots, peeled and diced
- 2 celery stalks, diced
- 1 large potato, peeled and diced
- 1 zucchini, diced
- 1/2 cup dried chickpeas, soaked overnight (or canned chickpeas, drained and rinsed)
- 6 cups vegetable or chicken broth
- 1 teaspoon ground cumin
- 1 teaspoon ground coriander
- 1/2 teaspoon turmeric
- 1/4 teaspoon ground cinnamon
- Salt and pepper to taste
- Fresh cilantro or parsley, chopped (for garnish)
- Lemon wedges (for serving)

Instructions:

In a large pot, heat the vegetable oil over medium heat. Add the chopped onion and cook until softened and translucent, about 5 minutes.
Add the minced garlic to the pot and cook for another minute, until fragrant.

Add the diced carrots, celery, potato, and zucchini to the pot. Cook for a few minutes, stirring occasionally.

Drain and rinse the soaked chickpeas (if using dried chickpeas) and add them to the pot.

Pour the vegetable or chicken broth into the pot, ensuring that all the vegetables and chickpeas are covered. If needed, add more water to cover.

Stir in the ground cumin, ground coriander, turmeric, ground cinnamon, salt, and pepper.

Bring the soup to a boil, then reduce the heat to low and let it simmer, partially covered, for about 45 minutes to 1 hour, or until the vegetables and chickpeas are tender.

Taste the soup and adjust the seasoning as needed, adding more salt and pepper if desired.

Once the soup is cooked and seasoned to your liking, remove it from heat.

Ladle the Yemenite soup into bowls and garnish with chopped fresh cilantro or parsley.

Serve the Marak Temani hot, with lemon wedges on the side for squeezing over the soup.

Enjoy this comforting and flavorful Yemenite soup as a satisfying meal on its own or as a starter to a larger feast!

Grilled eggplant with tahini sauce

Ingredients:

For the grilled eggplant:

- 2 medium-sized eggplants
- 2-3 tablespoons olive oil
- Salt and pepper to taste
- Optional: minced garlic, lemon juice, chopped parsley for extra flavor

For the tahini sauce:

- 1/4 cup tahini paste
- 2 tablespoons lemon juice
- 1 clove garlic, minced
- 2-4 tablespoons water, as needed
- Salt to taste

Optional toppings:

- Chopped fresh parsley or cilantro
- Toasted pine nuts
- Sumac
- Pomegranate seeds

Instructions:

Preheat your grill or grill pan over medium-high heat.

Slice the eggplants into rounds, about 1/2 inch thick. If desired, you can also slice them lengthwise into planks.

Brush both sides of the eggplant slices with olive oil and season with salt and pepper. If using minced garlic, you can sprinkle it over the eggplant slices for extra flavor.

Place the eggplant slices on the preheated grill and cook for 4-5 minutes on each side, or until they are tender and grill marks appear.

While the eggplant is grilling, prepare the tahini sauce. In a small bowl, whisk together the tahini paste, lemon juice, minced garlic, and a pinch of salt. Gradually add water, 1 tablespoon at a time, until the sauce reaches your desired consistency. The tahini sauce should be smooth and creamy.

Taste the tahini sauce and adjust the seasoning, adding more lemon juice or salt if needed.

Once the eggplant slices are grilled to your liking, remove them from the grill and arrange them on a serving platter.

Drizzle the tahini sauce over the grilled eggplant slices.

Garnish the dish with chopped fresh parsley or cilantro, toasted pine nuts, sumac, or pomegranate seeds, if desired.

Serve the grilled eggplant with tahini sauce immediately, while it's still warm.

Enjoy the delicious combination of smoky grilled eggplant and creamy tahini sauce!

Roasted red pepper spread (Muhammara)

Ingredients:

- 3 large red bell peppers
- 1 cup walnuts, toasted
- 1/2 cup breadcrumbs (you can use fresh breadcrumbs or store-bought)
- 2 cloves garlic, minced
- 2 tablespoons lemon juice
- 2 tablespoons pomegranate molasses (substitute with honey or maple syrup if unavailable)
- 1 teaspoon ground cumin
- 1 teaspoon smoked paprika
- 1/2 teaspoon cayenne pepper (adjust to taste)
- Salt and pepper to taste
- 1/4 cup extra virgin olive oil, plus more for drizzling
- Chopped fresh parsley or cilantro, for garnish (optional)
- Toasted sesame seeds or pine nuts, for garnish (optional)

Instructions:

Preheat your oven to broil (or grill) setting. Place the red bell peppers on a baking sheet lined with aluminum foil.

Broil the red bell peppers in the oven, turning occasionally, until they are charred and blistered on all sides, about 20-25 minutes.

Remove the peppers from the oven and transfer them to a bowl. Cover the bowl with plastic wrap and let the peppers steam for about 10 minutes. This will make it easier to peel off the skins.

Once the peppers are cool enough to handle, peel off the charred skins and remove the seeds and membranes. Discard the skins and seeds, and chop the roasted peppers into smaller pieces.

In a food processor, combine the roasted red peppers, toasted walnuts, breadcrumbs, minced garlic, lemon juice, pomegranate molasses, ground cumin, smoked paprika, cayenne pepper, salt, and pepper.

Process the mixture until smooth and well combined, scraping down the sides of the food processor as needed.

With the food processor running, slowly drizzle in the olive oil until the mixture is thick and creamy.

Taste the Muhammara and adjust the seasoning, adding more salt, pepper, lemon juice, or spices if needed.

Transfer the Muhammara to a serving bowl and drizzle with a little extra olive oil.

Garnish the Muhammara with chopped fresh parsley or cilantro, and toasted sesame seeds or pine nuts, if desired.

Serve the Muhammara at room temperature or chilled, with pita bread, crackers, or vegetable sticks for dipping.

Enjoy the rich and flavorful roasted red pepper spread (Muhammara)!

Grilled halloumi cheese

Ingredients:

- 1 block of halloumi cheese, sliced into 1/4 to 1/2 inch thick slices
- Olive oil, for brushing
- Optional: Fresh herbs (such as oregano or thyme), chili flakes, or lemon wedges for serving

Instructions:

Preheat your grill or grill pan over medium-high heat. If using an outdoor grill, lightly oil the grates to prevent the halloumi from sticking.
Brush both sides of the halloumi slices with olive oil. This will help prevent sticking and promote browning.
Once the grill is hot, place the halloumi slices directly onto the grill grates. You can also use a grill basket or grill mat if you prefer.
Grill the halloumi slices for 2-3 minutes on each side, or until they develop grill marks and turn golden brown.
Use a spatula to carefully flip the halloumi slices and grill the other side for an additional 2-3 minutes.
Once the halloumi is grilled to your liking and has developed a golden crust, remove it from the grill and transfer it to a serving platter.
Optionally, sprinkle the grilled halloumi with fresh herbs, chili flakes, or serve it with lemon wedges for squeezing over the cheese.
Serve the grilled halloumi cheese immediately while it's still warm.

Enjoy the deliciously salty and crispy grilled halloumi cheese as a standalone appetizer, as part of a mezze platter, or as a topping for salads or sandwiches!

Bulgarian-style cheese pastries (Börek)

Ingredients:

For the filling:

- 2 cups crumbled feta cheese
- 1 cup shredded mozzarella cheese
- 1/2 cup plain Greek yogurt
- 2 eggs
- 1/4 cup chopped fresh parsley
- Salt and pepper to taste

For assembly:

- 1 package of phyllo dough (about 12 sheets), thawed if frozen
- 1/2 cup unsalted butter, melted
- Sesame seeds or nigella seeds for topping (optional)

Instructions:

Preheat your oven to 375°F (190°C). Grease a baking sheet or line it with parchment paper.
In a mixing bowl, combine the crumbled feta cheese, shredded mozzarella cheese, Greek yogurt, eggs, chopped fresh parsley, salt, and pepper. Mix well until all the ingredients are evenly incorporated.
Lay out one sheet of phyllo dough on a clean work surface. Brush the entire sheet with melted butter.

Place another sheet of phyllo dough on top of the first sheet and brush it with melted butter as well. Repeat this process with 4-6 more sheets of phyllo dough, brushing each sheet with melted butter.

Spoon a portion of the cheese filling along the shorter edge of the phyllo dough, leaving a border of about 1 inch on the sides.

Roll the phyllo dough over the filling to form a log or cylinder. Tuck in the sides as you roll to enclose the filling completely.

Transfer the rolled pastry onto the prepared baking sheet, seam side down.

Repeat the process with the remaining phyllo dough and cheese filling until all the filling is used.

Brush the tops of the pastries with melted butter and sprinkle with sesame seeds or nigella seeds, if desired.

Bake the Börek in the preheated oven for 25-30 minutes, or until golden brown and crispy.

Remove the pastries from the oven and let them cool slightly before serving.

Serve the Bulgarian-style cheese pastries (Börek) warm or at room temperature as a delicious snack or appetizer.

Enjoy the rich and flavorful cheese-filled pastries, perfect for any occasion!

Sweet potato pancakes

Ingredients:

- 1 cup mashed sweet potato (cooked and peeled)
- 1 cup all-purpose flour
- 1 tablespoon brown sugar (or granulated sugar)
- 1 teaspoon baking powder
- 1/2 teaspoon baking soda
- 1/2 teaspoon ground cinnamon
- 1/4 teaspoon ground nutmeg
- 1/4 teaspoon salt
- 1 cup milk (or buttermilk)
- 1 large egg
- 2 tablespoons melted butter (or vegetable oil)
- 1 teaspoon vanilla extract
- Butter or oil for greasing the skillet

Optional toppings:

- Maple syrup
- Greek yogurt
- Chopped nuts (such as pecans or walnuts)
- Fresh berries
- Whipped cream

Instructions:

In a large mixing bowl, combine the mashed sweet potato, flour, brown sugar, baking powder, baking soda, cinnamon, nutmeg, and salt. Mix well to combine.

In a separate bowl, whisk together the milk, egg, melted butter (or oil), and vanilla extract until smooth.

Pour the wet ingredients into the dry ingredients and stir until just combined. Be careful not to overmix; a few lumps are okay.

Heat a skillet or griddle over medium heat and lightly grease with butter or oil.

Pour about 1/4 cup of batter onto the skillet for each pancake, using the back of a spoon to spread it into a round shape.

Cook the pancakes for 2-3 minutes, or until bubbles form on the surface and the edges look set.

Flip the pancakes and cook for an additional 1-2 minutes on the other side, or until golden brown and cooked through.

Transfer the cooked pancakes to a plate and keep them warm in a low oven while you cook the remaining pancakes.

Serve the sweet potato pancakes warm with your choice of toppings, such as maple syrup, Greek yogurt, chopped nuts, fresh berries, or whipped cream.

Enjoy these fluffy and flavorful sweet potato pancakes for a delightful breakfast treat!

Matbucha (Tomato and roasted pepper salad)

Ingredients:

- 4 large tomatoes, chopped
- 2 red bell peppers
- 2 green bell peppers
- 3 cloves garlic, minced
- 1-2 red chili peppers, seeded and finely chopped (adjust to taste)
- 2 tablespoons olive oil
- 1 teaspoon paprika
- 1/2 teaspoon ground cumin
- 1/2 teaspoon ground coriander
- Salt and pepper to taste
- Chopped fresh parsley or cilantro for garnish (optional)

Instructions:

Preheat your oven to broil (or grill) setting. Place the red and green bell peppers on a baking sheet lined with aluminum foil.
Broil the bell peppers in the oven, turning occasionally, until they are charred and blistered on all sides, about 20-25 minutes.
Remove the peppers from the oven and transfer them to a bowl. Cover the bowl with plastic wrap and let the peppers steam for about 10 minutes. This will make it easier to peel off the skins.
Once the peppers are cool enough to handle, peel off the charred skins, remove the seeds and membranes, and chop the roasted peppers into small pieces.
In a large skillet or saucepan, heat olive oil over medium heat. Add the minced garlic and chopped chili peppers, and sauté for 1-2 minutes until fragrant.

Add the chopped tomatoes to the skillet and cook for 5-7 minutes, stirring occasionally, until they start to break down and release their juices.

Stir in the chopped roasted peppers, paprika, ground cumin, ground coriander, salt, and pepper.

Reduce the heat to low and simmer the mixture for about 20-25 minutes, stirring occasionally, until it thickens and becomes jam-like in consistency.

Taste the Matbucha and adjust the seasoning, adding more salt, pepper, or spices if needed.

Once the Matbucha is cooked to your liking, remove it from heat and let it cool slightly.

Transfer the Matbucha to a serving bowl and garnish with chopped fresh parsley or cilantro, if desired.

Serve the Matbucha warm or at room temperature as a salad or side dish.

Enjoy the rich and flavorful Matbucha as a delicious addition to your meals!

Israeli cheese platter with olives and nuts

Ingredients:

- Assorted Israeli cheeses (Tzfatit, Labneh, Boukovo, Israeli Goat Cheese)
- Olives (Kalamata, green, mixed marinated)
- Nuts (almonds, walnuts, cashews, pistachios)
- Fresh fruit (apples, grapes, figs)
- Dried fruit (apricots, dates, figs)
- Crackers and breadsticks
- Honey or fruit jam
- Fresh herbs (basil, thyme, rosemary)

Instructions:

Arrange the Cheeses: Begin by arranging the assorted Israeli cheeses on a large serving platter or wooden board, leaving space between each variety.
Prepare the Accompaniments: Fill small bowls or ramekins with olives, nuts, honey, or fruit jam. Place them strategically around the cheeses on the platter.
Add Fresh and Dried Fruit: Scatter fresh fruit such as sliced apples, grapes, and figs, as well as dried fruit like apricots, dates, and figs, around the platter to complement the cheeses.
Arrange Crackers and Breadsticks: Arrange a selection of crackers and breadsticks in between the cheeses and other accompaniments, creating a balanced spread.
Garnish with Fresh Herbs: Garnish the platter with sprigs of fresh herbs such as basil, thyme, or rosemary for an elegant finishing touch.
Serve and Enjoy: Present the Israeli cheese platter with olives and nuts as a centerpiece for gatherings or as a delightful appetizer before a meal. Encourage guests to mix and match the cheeses with the various accompaniments for a burst of flavors and textures.

Notes:

- Feel free to customize the cheese platter based on personal preferences and availability of ingredients.
- Experiment with different combinations of cheeses, olives, nuts, and fruits to create a diverse and appealing spread.
- Serve the cheese platter with a variety of beverages such as wine, beer, or sparkling water to complement the flavors.

Iraqi-style stuffed vegetables (Dolma)

Ingredients:

For the stuffing:

- 1 cup long-grain rice, rinsed
- 250 grams ground beef or lamb
- 1 small onion, finely chopped
- 2 cloves garlic, minced
- 1/4 cup chopped fresh parsley
- 1/4 cup chopped fresh mint
- 1/4 cup chopped fresh dill
- 1 teaspoon ground cumin
- 1 teaspoon ground coriander
- Salt and pepper to taste
- 1 tablespoon tomato paste
- Juice of 1 lemon

For the vegetables:

- 8-10 medium-sized vegetables for stuffing, such as zucchini, eggplant, bell peppers, tomatoes, or onions
- Olive oil for drizzling

For the cooking liquid:

- 4 cups vegetable or chicken broth
- Juice of 1 lemon
- 2 tablespoons tomato paste
- Salt and pepper to taste

Instructions:

Prepare the vegetables: If using zucchini or eggplant, cut them in half lengthwise and scoop out the flesh, leaving a shell for stuffing. If using bell peppers or tomatoes, cut off the tops and remove the seeds and membranes. If using onions, peel and cut off the tops, then carefully remove the inner layers to create a hollow space for stuffing.

Prepare the stuffing: In a large mixing bowl, combine the rinsed rice, ground beef or lamb, chopped onion, minced garlic, chopped herbs (parsley, mint, and dill), ground cumin, ground coriander, salt, pepper, tomato paste, and lemon juice. Mix well to combine.

Stuff the vegetables: Stuff each prepared vegetable with the rice and meat mixture, filling them about 3/4 full. Press the stuffing gently into the vegetables to ensure they are well-packed.

Arrange in a pot: Place the stuffed vegetables in a large pot, arranging them snugly and upright. If there is any leftover stuffing, you can place it around the vegetables in the pot.

Prepare the cooking liquid: In a separate bowl, mix together the vegetable or chicken broth, lemon juice, tomato paste, salt, and pepper. Pour the mixture over the stuffed vegetables in the pot.

Cook the Dolma: Place the pot over medium heat and bring the liquid to a simmer. Once simmering, reduce the heat to low, cover the pot, and let the Dolma cook for about 45-60 minutes, or until the rice is cooked and the vegetables are tender.

Serve: Once cooked, carefully transfer the stuffed vegetables to a serving platter using a slotted spoon. Drizzle with a little olive oil and serve hot.

Notes:

- You can also add dried fruits like raisins or currants to the stuffing mixture for extra sweetness.
- Dolma can be served on its own as a main dish or as part of a mezze spread with other Middle Eastern dishes.
- Leftover Dolma can be stored in an airtight container in the refrigerator for up to 3-4 days.

Moroccan-style mint tea

Ingredients:

- 3-4 teaspoons loose Moroccan green tea leaves (gunpowder tea)
- 4 cups water
- 1 large bunch fresh mint leaves (about 1 cup packed)
- Sugar to taste (optional)
- Fresh lemon wedges (optional)

Instructions:

Rinse the tea leaves: Place the loose Moroccan green tea leaves in a tea strainer or a teapot. Rinse the tea leaves with a small amount of hot water and then discard the water. This helps to remove any dust and bitterness from the tea.
Brew the tea: In a large teapot, bring 4 cups of water to a boil. Once boiling, pour a small amount of the hot water over the tea leaves to cover them. Allow the tea leaves to steep for about 30 seconds, then discard this first infusion.
Add mint and sugar: To the teapot, add the fresh mint leaves and sugar to taste (if using). Traditionally, Moroccan mint tea is sweetened with a generous amount of sugar, but you can adjust the sweetness according to your preference or omit it entirely.
Brew again: Pour the remaining hot water over the mint leaves and sugar in the teapot. Cover the teapot and let the tea steep for about 3-5 minutes, depending on your desired strength of tea.
Strain and serve: After steeping, pour the tea through a fine-mesh strainer or a tea strainer into tea glasses. This will remove the tea leaves and any small mint particles, ensuring a clear tea.
Serve: Serve Moroccan mint tea hot and enjoy its refreshing flavor. You can accompany the tea with fresh lemon wedges on the side for squeezing into the tea, if desired.

Tips:

- Moroccan mint tea is traditionally served in small glasses with decorative tea glasses being commonly used in Morocco.
- To achieve the characteristic froth on top of Moroccan mint tea, pour the tea from a height into the glasses or use a pouring technique that creates bubbles.

- Adjust the sweetness of the tea according to your taste preferences. You can also use honey or other sweeteners instead of sugar.
- Moroccan mint tea is often enjoyed as part of a social gathering or as a way to welcome guests. It is also commonly served after meals to aid digestion.
- Experiment with the ratio of tea leaves to mint leaves and adjust it according to your taste preferences. Some people prefer a stronger tea flavor, while others prefer a more pronounced mint flavor.

Za'atar bread

Ingredients:

For the dough:

- 2 cups all-purpose flour
- 1 teaspoon instant yeast
- 1 teaspoon sugar
- 1 teaspoon salt
- 1 tablespoon olive oil
- 3/4 cup warm water

For the topping:

- 2-3 tablespoons za'atar spice blend
- 2-3 tablespoons olive oil

Instructions:

Prepare the dough: In a large mixing bowl, combine the all-purpose flour, instant yeast, sugar, and salt. Mix well to combine.

Make a well in the center of the dry ingredients and pour in the olive oil and warm water. Mix until a dough forms.

Transfer the dough to a lightly floured surface and knead it for about 5-7 minutes, or until it becomes smooth and elastic. Add more flour if the dough is too sticky, or a little water if it's too dry.

Place the dough in a greased bowl, cover it with a clean kitchen towel, and let it rise in a warm place for about 1 hour, or until doubled in size.

Preheat the oven: While the dough is rising, preheat your oven to 400°F (200°C). If you have a pizza stone, place it in the oven to preheat as well.

Shape the dough: Once the dough has doubled in size, punch it down to release the air bubbles. Divide the dough into two equal portions. Roll out each portion into a thin circle or oval shape, about 1/4 inch thick.

Top with za'atar: Place the rolled-out dough onto a parchment-lined baking sheet or directly onto the preheated pizza stone if using. Brush the surface of each dough round with olive oil, then sprinkle generously with za'atar spice blend, pressing lightly to adhere the za'atar to the dough.

Bake the bread: Transfer the baking sheet or pizza stone to the preheated oven and bake the za'atar bread for 12-15 minutes, or until golden brown and cooked through.

Serve: Remove the za'atar bread from the oven and let it cool slightly before slicing and serving. Enjoy the bread warm or at room temperature as a delicious snack or accompaniment to your favorite Middle Eastern dishes.

Note:

- Za'atar spice blend typically includes dried thyme, sumac, sesame seeds, and salt. You can find it at Middle Eastern grocery stores or make your own blend at home. Adjust the amount of za'atar according to your taste preferences.

Tunisian-style spicy carrot salad (Salata Meshwiya)

Ingredients:

- 1 lb carrots, peeled and sliced into thin rounds
- 2 red bell peppers
- 2-3 cloves garlic, minced
- 2 tablespoons olive oil
- 1-2 tablespoons harissa paste (adjust to taste)
- 1 tablespoon lemon juice
- Salt and pepper to taste
- Chopped fresh cilantro or parsley for garnish (optional)

Instructions:

Roast the red peppers: Preheat your oven to broil (or grill) setting. Place the red bell peppers on a baking sheet lined with aluminum foil. Broil the peppers in the oven, turning occasionally, until they are charred and blistered on all sides, about 20-25 minutes. Remove the peppers from the oven and transfer them to a bowl. Cover the bowl with plastic wrap and let the peppers steam for about 10 minutes. Once cooled, peel off the charred skins, remove the seeds and membranes, and chop the roasted peppers into small pieces.

Steam the carrots: While the peppers are roasting, steam the sliced carrots until they are tender but still crisp. This usually takes about 5-7 minutes. Once cooked, drain the carrots and set them aside to cool slightly.

Prepare the dressing: In a small bowl, whisk together the minced garlic, olive oil, harissa paste, lemon juice, salt, and pepper until well combined.

Combine the salad: In a large mixing bowl, combine the steamed carrots and chopped roasted red peppers. Pour the dressing over the vegetables and toss until evenly coated.

Chill and serve: Cover the salad and refrigerate it for at least 30 minutes to allow the flavors to meld together. Before serving, garnish the salad with chopped fresh cilantro or parsley, if desired.

Serve: Salata Meshwiya can be served as a side dish or appetizer. Enjoy it cold or at room temperature alongside your favorite Tunisian or Mediterranean dishes.

Note: Adjust the amount of harissa paste according to your desired level of spiciness. You can also add other ingredients like olives, capers, or preserved lemon for additional flavor.

Turkish coffee

Ingredients:

- Freshly ground Turkish coffee beans (finely ground)
- Cold water
- Sugar (optional)

Equipment:

- Turkish coffee pot (cezve or ibrik)
- Small coffee cups (demitasse cups)

Instructions:

Measure the water: For each cup of Turkish coffee, measure out one cup of cold water using the coffee cup you plan to serve the coffee in.

Grind the coffee: Grind the coffee beans to a very fine consistency, almost like powder. Traditional Turkish coffee requires a very fine grind to achieve the desired texture and flavor.

Add the coffee to the pot: Place the finely ground coffee into the Turkish coffee pot, using about one heaping teaspoon of coffee for each cup of water.

Add sugar (optional): If you prefer your coffee sweetened, add sugar to taste to the coffee grounds in the pot before adding water. Traditionally, Turkish coffee is often brewed with sugar already added.

Add water: Pour the cold water into the coffee pot, stirring gently to combine the coffee and water. Place the pot on the stove over low to medium heat.

Brew the coffee: Allow the coffee to come to a gentle boil, watching carefully to prevent it from boiling over. As the coffee heats up, a thick foam will begin to form on the surface. This foam is an essential part of Turkish coffee and adds to its unique texture.

Simmer: Once the coffee comes to a boil and the foam forms, reduce the heat to low and simmer the coffee for about 1-2 minutes, allowing the flavors to develop further.

Serve: Carefully pour the brewed coffee into the small coffee cups, making sure to distribute the foam evenly among the cups. Serve the coffee hot and enjoy it slowly, savoring its rich flavor and aroma.

Note: Turkish coffee is typically served without milk, but you can add a small amount of milk if desired. It is also customary to serve Turkish coffee with a glass of water to cleanse the palate between sips. Enjoy your authentic Turkish coffee experience!

Armenian cucumber yogurt salad (Jajik)

Ingredients:

- 2 medium Armenian cucumbers (or 1 English cucumber), finely chopped or grated

- 1 cup plain Greek yogurt
- 1-2 cloves garlic, minced
- 2 tablespoons fresh mint, finely chopped
- 1 tablespoon fresh dill, finely chopped
- 1 tablespoon fresh parsley, finely chopped
- 1 tablespoon extra virgin olive oil
- 1 tablespoon lemon juice
- Salt and pepper to taste
- Optional: 1/4 teaspoon ground sumac for garnish

Instructions:

Prepare the cucumbers: If using Armenian cucumbers, peel them and remove the seeds if they are large. Finely chop the cucumbers or grate them using a box grater. If using English cucumbers, simply chop or grate them without peeling.

Combine ingredients: In a large mixing bowl, combine the chopped cucumbers, Greek yogurt, minced garlic, chopped mint, dill, and parsley. Mix well to combine.

Season: Add the extra virgin olive oil, lemon juice, salt, and pepper to taste. Stir until all the ingredients are evenly distributed.

Chill: Cover the bowl and refrigerate the Jajik for at least 30 minutes to allow the flavors to meld together and for the salad to chill.

Serve: Once chilled, give the Jajik a final stir and taste for seasoning, adjusting as needed. Transfer the salad to a serving bowl and sprinkle with ground sumac for garnish, if desired.

Enjoy: Serve the Armenian cucumber yogurt salad (Jajik) as a refreshing side dish or appetizer. It pairs well with grilled meats, kebabs, or as part of a mezze spread.

Note: Jajik can be stored in the refrigerator for up to 2-3 days. Give it a stir before serving leftovers, as the liquid from the cucumbers and yogurt may separate slightly.

Tunisian-style fried egg with spicy tomato sauce (Ojja)

Ingredients:

- 4 large eggs
- 2 tablespoons olive oil
- 1 onion, finely chopped

- 2 cloves garlic, minced
- 2 red bell peppers, diced
- 2 ripe tomatoes, chopped
- 1 tablespoon tomato paste
- 1 teaspoon paprika
- 1/2 teaspoon cumin
- 1/2 teaspoon cayenne pepper (adjust to taste)
- Salt and pepper to taste
- Fresh parsley or cilantro for garnish
- Crusty bread for serving

Instructions:

Prepare the sauce: Heat olive oil in a large skillet over medium heat. Add the chopped onion and cook until softened, about 3-4 minutes. Add the minced garlic and cook for another minute until fragrant.

Add the peppers and tomatoes: Add the diced red bell peppers to the skillet and cook for 5-6 minutes until they begin to soften. Then add the chopped tomatoes and tomato paste to the skillet. Stir well to combine.

Season the sauce: Season the sauce with paprika, cumin, cayenne pepper, salt, and pepper. Stir to evenly distribute the spices. Allow the sauce to simmer over medium-low heat for about 10-15 minutes, stirring occasionally, until it thickens slightly.

Make wells for the eggs: Once the sauce has thickened, use a spoon to create wells in the sauce for the eggs. Crack the eggs one at a time and gently place them into the wells in the sauce.

Cook the eggs: Cover the skillet and let the eggs cook for about 5-7 minutes, or until the egg whites are set but the yolks are still runny. If you prefer your eggs more well-done, cook them for a few minutes longer.

Garnish and serve: Once the eggs are cooked to your liking, remove the skillet from the heat. Garnish the Ojja with fresh parsley or cilantro. Serve the Ojja hot with crusty bread for dipping.

Enjoy: Serve the Tunisian-style fried egg with spicy tomato sauce (Ojja) as a hearty breakfast or brunch dish. Enjoy the flavorful sauce and runny egg yolks with crusty bread for a delicious and satisfying meal.

Note: Adjust the level of spiciness according to your taste preferences by adding more or less cayenne pepper. You can also customize the dish by adding other vegetables or spices to the sauce.

Iraqi-style date cookies (Kleicha)

Ingredients:

For the dough:

- 3 cups all-purpose flour
- 1 cup unsalted butter, softened
- 1/2 cup granulated sugar

- 1/2 cup warm milk
- 1 teaspoon active dry yeast
- 1/4 teaspoon salt
- 1 teaspoon ground cardamom
- 1 teaspoon ground mahlab (optional, for added flavor)

For the date filling:

- 2 cups pitted dates, chopped
- 2 tablespoons unsalted butter
- 1 teaspoon ground cinnamon
- 1/4 teaspoon ground cloves
- 1/4 teaspoon ground nutmeg
- 1/4 cup water

For garnish (optional):

- Sesame seeds or powdered sugar for sprinkling on top

Instructions:

Prepare the dough:
- In a small bowl, dissolve the yeast in the warm milk and let it sit for about 5-10 minutes until frothy.
- In a large mixing bowl, cream together the softened butter and sugar until light and fluffy.
- Add the activated yeast mixture to the butter-sugar mixture and mix well.
- Gradually add the flour, salt, ground cardamom, and ground mahlab (if using) to the wet ingredients. Mix until a smooth dough forms. You may need to knead the dough lightly with your hands to incorporate all the flour.

Make the date filling:
- In a saucepan, combine the chopped dates, butter, ground cinnamon, ground cloves, ground nutmeg, and water.
- Cook the mixture over medium heat, stirring frequently, until the dates are soft and the mixture has thickened into a paste-like consistency. Remove from heat and let it cool slightly.

Assemble the cookies:
- Preheat your oven to 350°F (175°C) and line a baking sheet with parchment paper.

- Divide the dough into small portions and roll each portion into a ball.
- Flatten each dough ball into a small disc or circle with your fingers or a rolling pin.
- Place a small amount of the date filling in the center of each dough circle.
- Fold the edges of the dough over the filling and pinch to seal, shaping the cookies into crescent or oval shapes.

Bake the cookies:

- Place the filled cookies on the prepared baking sheet, leaving some space between them.
- If desired, sprinkle sesame seeds on top of the cookies for garnish.
- Bake in the preheated oven for 15-20 minutes, or until the cookies are golden brown.

Cool and serve:

- Remove the Kleicha from the oven and let them cool on the baking sheet for a few minutes before transferring them to a wire rack to cool completely.
- Once cooled, dust the cookies with powdered sugar if desired.
- Serve the Iraqi-style date cookies (Kleicha) as a sweet treat with tea or coffee.

Enjoy these delicious and aromatic Iraqi cookies, filled with flavorful date filling!

Cheese borek with filo pastry

Ingredients:

- 1 package (about 16 ounces) filo pastry sheets, thawed if frozen
- 2 cups crumbled feta cheese
- 1 cup shredded mozzarella cheese
- 1/2 cup grated Parmesan cheese
- 1/4 cup chopped fresh parsley
- 1/4 cup chopped fresh dill (optional)

- 2 eggs, lightly beaten
- 1/2 cup melted butter or olive oil
- Sesame seeds or nigella seeds for sprinkling (optional)

Instructions:

Preheat the oven: Preheat your oven to 350°F (175°C). Grease a baking sheet or line it with parchment paper.

Prepare the cheese filling: In a large mixing bowl, combine the crumbled feta cheese, shredded mozzarella cheese, grated Parmesan cheese, chopped parsley, and chopped dill (if using). Mix well to combine. Add the lightly beaten eggs and mix until the cheese mixture is evenly coated.

Assemble the börek:
- Lay out one sheet of filo pastry on a clean work surface. Brush the entire surface lightly with melted butter or olive oil.
- Place another sheet of filo pastry on top and brush it with melted butter or olive oil as well.
- Repeat this process until you have a stack of about 6-8 filo sheets.
- Spoon a generous portion of the cheese filling along one edge of the filo pastry stack, leaving a border of about 1 inch.
- Roll up the filo pastry tightly over the filling to form a long cylinder. Tuck in the edges as you roll to seal the börek.
- Place the rolled börek seam side down on the prepared baking sheet.

Bake the börek: Repeat the process with the remaining filo pastry sheets and cheese filling until all the börek are assembled. Brush the tops of the börek with more melted butter or olive oil and sprinkle with sesame seeds or nigella seeds, if desired.

**Bake in the preheated oven for 25-30 minutes, or until the börek are golden brown and crispy.

Serve: Remove the cheese börek from the oven and let them cool slightly before serving. Cut them into slices and serve warm as a delicious appetizer or snack.

Enjoy these crispy and savory cheese börek with filo pastry! They're perfect for sharing with family and friends or enjoying as a tasty treat anytime.

Yemenite bread (Jachnun) with grated tomato

Ingredients:

For the Jachnun:

- 500g (about 4 cups) all-purpose flour
- 1 teaspoon salt
- 1 teaspoon sugar
- 1/2 cup vegetable oil or melted butter

- 1 cup warm water
- Additional vegetable oil or melted butter, for brushing

For serving:

- 4-5 ripe tomatoes
- Salt, to taste
- Ground black pepper, to taste
- Ground cumin, to taste
- Ground paprika or cayenne pepper, to taste
- Chopped fresh parsley, for garnish (optional)

Instructions:

Prepare the dough:
- In a large mixing bowl, combine the all-purpose flour, salt, and sugar. Gradually add the vegetable oil or melted butter and warm water, mixing until a soft dough forms.
- Knead the dough on a lightly floured surface for about 5-7 minutes, or until smooth and elastic. Shape the dough into a ball.

Let the dough rest:
- Place the dough ball in a greased bowl, cover it with a clean kitchen towel or plastic wrap, and let it rest at room temperature for at least 1 hour, or until it doubles in size.

Shape the Jachnun:
- Preheat your oven to 250°C (480°F).
- Divide the rested dough into 8 equal portions. Roll each portion into a ball and flatten it slightly with your hands.
- Brush each flattened dough round generously with vegetable oil or melted butter.
- Roll up each dough round into a tight cylinder, similar to a cinnamon roll, and place it seam side down on a baking sheet lined with parchment paper.

Bake the Jachnun:
- Place the baking sheet in the preheated oven and bake the Jachnun for about 15-20 minutes, or until golden brown and crispy on the outside.

Prepare the grated tomato:
- While the Jachnun is baking, grate the ripe tomatoes using a box grater. Discard the skins and excess liquid.

- Season the grated tomato with salt, ground black pepper, ground cumin, and ground paprika or cayenne pepper, to taste.

Serve:
- Once the Jachnun is baked and crispy, remove it from the oven and let it cool slightly.
- Serve the Jachnun warm with the grated tomato mixture on the side.
- Garnish with chopped fresh parsley, if desired.

Enjoy the delicious Yemenite bread (Jachnun) with grated tomato as a traditional Yemeni Jewish breakfast dish, typically served on Shabbat mornings.

Turkish-style stuffed peppers (Biber Dolması)

Ingredients:

- 6 large bell peppers (any color)
- 1 cup long-grain rice, rinsed
- 250g ground beef or lamb
- 1 onion, finely chopped
- 2 tomatoes, finely chopped
- 2 tablespoons tomato paste

- 2 tablespoons olive oil
- 2 tablespoons pine nuts (optional)
- 2 tablespoons currants or raisins (optional)
- 2 teaspoons dried mint
- 1 teaspoon ground cumin
- 1 teaspoon paprika
- Salt and pepper to taste
- 2 cups hot water or beef broth
- Fresh parsley or mint leaves for garnish

Instructions:

Prepare the peppers:
- Cut the tops off the bell peppers and remove the seeds and membranes. Rinse the peppers under cold water and set them aside.

Prepare the filling:
- In a large bowl, combine the rinsed rice, ground meat, finely chopped onion, chopped tomatoes, tomato paste, olive oil, pine nuts (if using), currants or raisins (if using), dried mint, ground cumin, paprika, salt, and pepper. Mix well to combine.

Stuff the peppers:
- Stuff each bell pepper with the rice and meat mixture, pressing it down gently to fill the peppers evenly. Leave a little space at the top to allow the rice to expand during cooking.

Cook the stuffed peppers:
- Place the stuffed peppers in a large pot, standing them upright. Arrange them snugly to prevent them from falling over.
- Pour the hot water or beef broth into the pot around the peppers, making sure not to pour it over the tops of the peppers.
- Cover the pot with a lid and bring the liquid to a boil over medium-high heat. Once boiling, reduce the heat to low and let the peppers simmer gently for about 30-40 minutes, or until the rice is cooked and the peppers are tender.

Serve:
- Once cooked, transfer the stuffed peppers to a serving platter using a slotted spoon. Spoon some of the cooking liquid over the peppers.
- Garnish the stuffed peppers with fresh parsley or mint leaves.
- Serve hot as a main dish or part of a mezze spread, along with yogurt or a salad on the side.

Enjoy these delicious Turkish-style stuffed peppers (Biber Dolması) filled with a savory rice and meat mixture!

Moroccan-style semolina pancakes (Baghrir)

Ingredients:

- 1 cup fine semolina
- 1/2 cup all-purpose flour
- 1 teaspoon active dry yeast
- 1 teaspoon sugar
- 1/2 teaspoon salt
- 2 cups lukewarm water
- 1 teaspoon baking powder
- Butter or oil for greasing the pan

Instructions:

Prepare the batter:
- In a large mixing bowl, combine the fine semolina, all-purpose flour, active dry yeast, sugar, and salt.
- Gradually pour in the lukewarm water while whisking continuously to avoid lumps. Mix until you have a smooth batter.
- Cover the bowl with a clean kitchen towel and let the batter rest for about 30 minutes to allow the yeast to activate.

Cook the pancakes:
- After the resting period, you'll notice that the batter has slightly risen and developed bubbles on the surface.
- Stir in the baking powder into the batter. The batter will become slightly thinner.
- Heat a non-stick skillet or griddle over medium heat. Lightly grease the surface with butter or oil.
- Pour about 1/4 cup of the batter onto the skillet to form a pancake, using a ladle or measuring cup to spread it evenly.
- Cook the pancake for about 2-3 minutes, or until bubbles start to form on the surface and the edges look set.
- Baghrir is only cooked on one side, so there's no need to flip it. The surface should be covered with "eyes" or holes formed by the bubbles.

Serve:
- Repeat the process with the remaining batter, stacking the cooked pancakes on a plate.
- Serve the Baghrir warm with your choice of toppings, such as honey, melted butter, jam, or syrup.
- Baghrir can also be served with a sprinkle of powdered sugar or a drizzle of argan oil for an authentic Moroccan touch.

Enjoy these light and fluffy Moroccan-style semolina pancakes (Baghrir) for a delightful breakfast or snack!

Georgian cheese bread (Khachapuri)

Ingredients:

For the dough:

- 3 cups all-purpose flour
- 1 teaspoon salt
- 1 teaspoon sugar
- 1 packet (2 1/4 teaspoons) active dry yeast
- 1 cup lukewarm milk
- 2 tablespoons olive oil or melted butter

For the filling:

- 2 cups grated cheese (a mix of mozzarella and feta works well)
- 1 cup crumbled feta cheese
- 1 cup grated Imeretian or Sulguni cheese (if available)
- 2 eggs
- 1/4 cup plain Greek yogurt or sour cream
- 2 tablespoons melted butter
- Salt and pepper to taste

Instructions:

Prepare the dough:
- In a large mixing bowl, combine the lukewarm milk, sugar, and active dry yeast. Let it sit for 5-10 minutes until foamy.
- Add the flour and salt to the yeast mixture, and knead until a smooth dough forms. If the dough is too sticky, add more flour, a little at a time.
- Place the dough in a greased bowl, cover it with a clean kitchen towel, and let it rise in a warm place for about 1 hour, or until doubled in size.

Make the filling:
- In a separate bowl, mix together the grated cheese, crumbled feta cheese, grated Imeretian or Sulguni cheese, eggs, Greek yogurt or sour cream, melted butter, salt, and pepper. Mix until well combined.

Assemble the Khachapuri:
- Preheat your oven to 450°F (230°C). Line a baking sheet with parchment paper.
- Punch down the risen dough and divide it into 4 equal portions.
- Roll out each portion of dough into an oval or rectangle shape, about 1/4 inch thick.
- Spoon a quarter of the cheese filling onto one half of each dough oval, leaving a border around the edges.
- Fold the other half of the dough over the filling and pinch the edges to seal, forming a boat-like shape.

Bake the Khachapuri:
- Transfer the filled Khachapuri to the prepared baking sheet.
- Bake in the preheated oven for 15-20 minutes, or until the crust is golden brown and the cheese is bubbly and melted.

Serve:
- Remove the Khachapuri from the oven and brush the tops with melted butter.
- Serve the Khachapuri hot, either whole or sliced into portions. Enjoy!

Khachapuri is best enjoyed fresh from the oven, while the cheese is still warm and gooey. Serve it as a main dish or as part of a spread of Georgian dishes for a delicious and comforting meal.

Date and walnut bread

Ingredients:

- 1 cup chopped dates
- 1 cup chopped walnuts
- 1 3/4 cups all-purpose flour
- 1 teaspoon baking powder
- 1/2 teaspoon baking soda
- 1/4 teaspoon salt
- 1/2 cup unsalted butter, softened
- 1/2 cup brown sugar
- 2 large eggs
- 1 teaspoon vanilla extract
- 1/2 cup plain yogurt or sour cream

Instructions:

Preheat your oven: Preheat the oven to 350°F (175°C). Grease a 9x5-inch loaf pan and line it with parchment paper, leaving some overhang on the sides for easy removal.

Prepare the dates and walnuts: In a small bowl, combine the chopped dates and walnuts. Toss them with a tablespoon of flour to coat (this will prevent them from sinking to the bottom of the bread).

Mix the dry ingredients: In a medium-sized bowl, whisk together the all-purpose flour, baking powder, baking soda, and salt. Set aside.

Cream the butter and sugar: In a large mixing bowl, cream together the softened butter and brown sugar until light and fluffy.

Add the eggs and vanilla: Beat in the eggs, one at a time, until well combined. Mix in the vanilla extract.

Add the dry ingredients: Gradually add the dry ingredients to the wet ingredients, mixing until just combined.

Add the yogurt or sour cream: Stir in the plain yogurt or sour cream until smooth and well incorporated.

Fold in the dates and walnuts: Gently fold the chopped dates and walnuts into the batter until evenly distributed.

Bake the bread: Pour the batter into the prepared loaf pan and smooth the top with a spatula. Bake in the preheated oven for 50-60 minutes, or until a toothpick inserted into the center comes out clean.

Cool and serve: Allow the bread to cool in the pan for 10 minutes before transferring it to a wire rack to cool completely. Once cooled, slice and serve the date and walnut bread. Enjoy!

This date and walnut bread is perfect for breakfast, brunch, or as a snack any time of day. The combination of sweet dates and crunchy walnuts makes for a delicious and satisfying treat.

Bulgarian-style yogurt with honey and nuts

Ingredients:

- Greek yogurt or Bulgarian yogurt
- Honey (to taste)
- Assorted nuts (such as walnuts, almonds, pistachios, or hazelnuts), chopped or crushed

Instructions:

Prepare the yogurt:
- If using Greek yogurt, you can use it directly from the container. If using Bulgarian yogurt, you may want to strain it through cheesecloth or a fine mesh sieve to achieve a thicker consistency similar to Greek yogurt.

Serve the yogurt:
- Spoon the desired amount of yogurt into serving bowls or cups.

Drizzle with honey:

- Drizzle honey over the yogurt to sweeten it to your taste. Start with a small amount and adjust according to your preference.

Add nuts:
- Sprinkle chopped or crushed nuts over the yogurt and honey. You can use a single type of nut or a combination of nuts for added flavor and texture.

Serve and enjoy:
- Serve the Bulgarian-style yogurt with honey and nuts immediately as a delicious and nutritious breakfast, snack, or dessert.

Variations:

- You can add other toppings such as fresh fruits (like berries or sliced bananas), granola, or coconut flakes for additional flavor and texture.
- For extra richness, you can mix the honey directly into the yogurt instead of drizzling it on top.
- Adjust the sweetness level by adding more or less honey according to your taste preferences.
- Toasting the nuts lightly before adding them to the yogurt can enhance their flavor.

This simple yet delicious combination of creamy yogurt, sweet honey, and crunchy nuts makes for a satisfying and nutritious snack or dessert that you can enjoy any time of the day.

Turkish-style spinach and feta borek

Ingredients:

- 1 package of phyllo pastry sheets, thawed if frozen
- 300g fresh spinach, washed and chopped
- 200g feta cheese, crumbled
- 1 onion, finely chopped
- 2 cloves garlic, minced
- 2 tablespoons olive oil
- 1 teaspoon paprika
- Salt and pepper to taste
- 2 eggs, beaten
- 1/4 cup milk
- 1/4 cup melted butter or olive oil, for brushing

Instructions:

Prepare the filling:

- Heat the olive oil in a large skillet over medium heat. Add the chopped onion and cook until softened, about 5 minutes.
- Add the minced garlic and cook for another minute until fragrant.
- Add the chopped spinach to the skillet and cook until wilted, about 2-3 minutes.
- Season the spinach mixture with paprika, salt, and pepper, to taste. Remove from heat and let it cool slightly.
- Once cooled, transfer the spinach mixture to a mixing bowl and stir in the crumbled feta cheese until well combined.

Assemble the borek:
- Preheat your oven to 350°F (175°C). Grease a baking dish with butter or oil.
- Lay one sheet of phyllo pastry on a clean work surface and brush it lightly with melted butter or oil. Place another sheet of phyllo pastry on top and brush it with butter or oil as well. Repeat this process with 4-5 sheets of phyllo pastry, stacking them on top of each other.
- Spread half of the spinach and feta filling evenly over the stacked phyllo pastry sheets, leaving a border around the edges.
- Roll up the phyllo pastry sheets tightly into a log, starting from one short end. Place the rolled borek seam side down in the prepared baking dish.
- Repeat the process with the remaining phyllo pastry sheets and filling to make a second borek.

Bake the borek:
- In a small bowl, whisk together the beaten eggs and milk. Pour the egg mixture evenly over the top of the borek.
- Bake in the preheated oven for 25-30 minutes, or until the borek is golden brown and crispy on top.

Serve:
- Remove the Turkish-style spinach and feta borek from the oven and let it cool slightly before slicing and serving.
- Enjoy the borek warm or at room temperature as a delicious appetizer, side dish, or snack.

This Turkish-style spinach and feta borek is a flavorful and satisfying dish that's perfect for any occasion. Enjoy its crispy layers and savory filling!

Moroccan-style orange and almond salad

Ingredients:

- 4 oranges, peeled and sliced into rounds or segments
- 1/4 cup sliced almonds, toasted
- 1/4 cup fresh cilantro or mint leaves, chopped
- 1/4 cup red onion, thinly sliced (optional)
- 1/4 cup pitted green olives, sliced (optional)

For the dressing:

- 2 tablespoons olive oil
- 1 tablespoon lemon juice
- 1 teaspoon honey or maple syrup
- 1/2 teaspoon ground cumin
- 1/4 teaspoon ground cinnamon
- Salt and pepper to taste

Instructions:

Prepare the oranges:
- Peel the oranges and remove any white pith. Slice them into rounds or segments, discarding any seeds. Place the sliced oranges in a large serving bowl.

Toast the almonds:
- In a dry skillet over medium heat, toast the sliced almonds until golden brown and fragrant, about 3-5 minutes. Stir frequently to prevent burning. Once toasted, remove the almonds from the skillet and let them cool.

Prepare the dressing:
- In a small bowl, whisk together the olive oil, lemon juice, honey or maple syrup, ground cumin, ground cinnamon, salt, and pepper until well combined.

Assemble the salad:
- Add the toasted almonds, chopped cilantro or mint leaves, sliced red onion (if using), and sliced green olives (if using) to the bowl with the sliced oranges.

Add the dressing:
- Pour the dressing over the salad ingredients in the bowl.

Toss gently:
- Gently toss all the ingredients together until the oranges are evenly coated with the dressing and the other ingredients are distributed throughout the salad.

Chill and serve:
- Cover the bowl with plastic wrap and refrigerate the salad for at least 30 minutes to allow the flavors to meld together.
- Serve the Moroccan-style orange and almond salad chilled as a refreshing side dish or appetizer.

This salad is bursting with flavor and makes a beautiful addition to any meal. Enjoy its vibrant colors and zesty Moroccan-inspired dressing!

Iraqi-style kubba (Stuffed bulgur wheat dumplings)

Ingredients:

For the dough:

- 2 cups fine bulgur wheat
- 1 cup boiling water
- 1 teaspoon salt

For the filling:

- 250g ground beef or lamb
- 1 onion, finely chopped
- 2 tablespoons olive oil
- 2 tablespoons pine nuts (optional)
- 1/2 teaspoon ground allspice
- 1/2 teaspoon ground cinnamon
- Salt and pepper to taste
- Chopped fresh parsley or cilantro for garnish (optional)

Instructions:

   Prepare the dough:

- Place the fine bulgur wheat in a large mixing bowl. Pour the boiling water over the bulgur wheat and let it sit for about 30 minutes to soften.
- After soaking, drain any excess water from the bulgur wheat using a fine mesh sieve or cheesecloth.
- Add salt to the drained bulgur wheat and knead it with your hands until you get a smooth dough-like consistency. If the dough feels too dry, you can add a little water, one tablespoon at a time, until it comes together.

Prepare the filling:
- In a skillet, heat the olive oil over medium heat. Add the chopped onion and sauté until translucent, about 3-4 minutes.
- Add the ground beef or lamb to the skillet and cook until browned, breaking it up with a spoon as it cooks.
- Stir in the pine nuts (if using), ground allspice, ground cinnamon, salt, and pepper. Cook for another 2-3 minutes, then remove the skillet from the heat and let the filling cool slightly.

Assemble the kubba:
- Take a small portion of the bulgur wheat dough and flatten it in the palm of your hand to form a small disc.
- Place a spoonful of the meat filling in the center of the disc.
- Fold the edges of the bulgur wheat dough over the filling, pinching them together to seal and form a ball or oval shape. You can wet your hands with water to help seal the edges if needed.
- Repeat the process with the remaining bulgur wheat dough and filling until you've used up all the ingredients.

Cook the kubba:
- Heat a large pot of water over medium heat until it reaches a gentle simmer.
- Carefully drop the stuffed bulgur wheat dumplings into the simmering water, one by one. Avoid overcrowding the pot.
- Let the kubba cook in the simmering water for about 15-20 minutes, or until they float to the surface and the bulgur wheat dough is cooked through.

Serve:
- Once cooked, remove the kubba from the pot using a slotted spoon and drain them on a plate lined with paper towels.
- Garnish the kubba with chopped fresh parsley or cilantro if desired, and serve them warm as a delicious appetizer or main dish.

Enjoy these Iraqi-style kubba, filled with flavorful meat and wrapped in a tender bulgur wheat dough!

Armenian-style apricot compote

Ingredients:

- 2 cups dried apricots
- 4 cups water
- 1 cup granulated sugar (adjust to taste)
- 1 cinnamon stick
- 3-4 whole cloves
- 1 teaspoon vanilla extract (optional)
- Juice of 1 lemon (optional)

Instructions:

Prepare the dried apricots:
- Rinse the dried apricots under cold water to remove any dust or debris. Drain well.

Make the sugar syrup:
- In a large saucepan, combine the water and granulated sugar. Stir until the sugar is dissolved.
- Add the cinnamon stick and whole cloves to the saucepan.

Simmer the apricots:
- Add the dried apricots to the saucepan with the sugar syrup.

- Bring the mixture to a boil over medium-high heat, then reduce the heat to low and let it simmer gently for about 20-25 minutes, or until the apricots are tender and plump.

Flavoring (optional):
- If desired, add vanilla extract to the compote for extra flavor. You can also add a squeeze of lemon juice to brighten the flavors.

Cool and serve:
- Once the apricots are tender and the compote has thickened slightly, remove the saucepan from the heat and let the compote cool to room temperature.
- Discard the cinnamon stick and whole cloves.

Chill (optional):
- You can serve the compote warm or chilled. If serving chilled, transfer the compote to a container and refrigerate for at least 1-2 hours before serving.

Serve:
- Serve the Armenian-style apricot compote in individual bowls or glasses, along with some of the syrup.
- You can enjoy the compote on its own as a dessert, or serve it with a dollop of whipped cream or Greek yogurt for added richness.

Storage:
- Store any leftover compote in an airtight container in the refrigerator for up to one week.

Armenian-style apricot compote is a delightful dessert with a perfect balance of sweetness and tartness, enhanced by the warm spices. Enjoy it as a refreshing treat on its own or as a topping for yogurt, ice cream, or pancakes.

Georgian-style walnut and red pepper dip (Adjika)

Ingredients:

- 1 cup walnuts, finely chopped
- 2 roasted red bell peppers, peeled and seeded
- 2 cloves garlic, minced
- 1 tablespoon red wine vinegar
- 1 tablespoon olive oil
- Salt to taste
- Fresh cilantro or parsley for garnish (optional)

Instructions:

Prepare the roasted red bell peppers:
- Preheat your oven to 400°F (200°C).
- Place the whole red bell peppers on a baking sheet and roast them in the preheated oven for about 20-25 minutes, or until the skins are charred and blistered.
- Remove the roasted peppers from the oven and transfer them to a bowl. Cover the bowl with plastic wrap or a kitchen towel and let the peppers steam for about 10 minutes.
- Once steamed, peel off the charred skins, remove the seeds, and chop the roasted peppers.

Make the dip:

- In a food processor or blender, combine the finely chopped walnuts, roasted red bell peppers, minced garlic, red wine vinegar, and olive oil.
- Blend the mixture until smooth and creamy. If the dip is too thick, you can add a little water or more olive oil to achieve the desired consistency.
- Season the dip with salt to taste and adjust any other seasonings as needed.

Serve:
- Transfer the walnut and red pepper dip to a serving bowl.
- Garnish with fresh cilantro or parsley, if desired.
- Serve the dip with bread, crackers, or vegetable sticks for dipping.

This Georgian-style walnut and red pepper dip is creamy, flavorful, and perfect for spreading on bread or using as a dip for your favorite snacks. Enjoy its rich taste and unique flavors!

Iraqi-style beef kebabs (Kebab Hindi)

Ingredients:

- 500g ground beef (preferably lean)
- 1 onion, finely chopped
- 2 cloves garlic, minced
- 2 tablespoons chopped fresh parsley
- 1 teaspoon ground cumin
- 1 teaspoon ground coriander
- 1/2 teaspoon paprika
- 1/2 teaspoon ground black pepper
- 1/2 teaspoon salt, or to taste
- 1 tablespoon vegetable oil, for brushing (if grilling)

Instructions:

Prepare the meat mixture:
- In a large mixing bowl, combine the ground beef, finely chopped onion, minced garlic, chopped fresh parsley, ground cumin, ground coriander, paprika, ground black pepper, and salt.
- Use your hands to mix all the ingredients together until well combined. Make sure the spices are evenly distributed throughout the meat mixture.

Shape the kebabs:
- Take a handful of the meat mixture and mold it onto skewers, forming elongated sausage-like shapes. Press the meat firmly onto the skewers to ensure they hold together during cooking.
- Repeat the process with the remaining meat mixture until all the skewers are filled.

Cook the kebabs:

- Grilling method: Preheat an outdoor grill or grill pan over medium-high heat. Brush the grill grates with vegetable oil to prevent sticking. Place the kebabs on the grill and cook for 4-6 minutes on each side, or until they are cooked through and nicely charred on the outside.
- Oven method: Preheat your oven to 400°F (200°C). Place the kebabs on a baking sheet lined with parchment paper. Bake in the preheated oven for 20-25 minutes, or until they are cooked through and browned.

Serve:
- Once cooked, remove the kebabs from the grill or oven and let them rest for a few minutes.
- Serve the Iraqi-style beef kebabs hot, either on their own or with your choice of sides such as rice, salad, or flatbread.

These Iraqi-style beef kebabs (Kebab Hindi) are packed with flavor and make a delicious and satisfying meal. Enjoy them as a main dish or as part of a Middle Eastern-inspired feast!

Turkish-style simit bread with sesame seeds

Ingredients:

- 3 1/2 cups all-purpose flour
- 1 tablespoon active dry yeast
- 1 teaspoon sugar
- 1 teaspoon salt
- 1 cup lukewarm water
- 2 tablespoons olive oil
- 1/4 cup molasses or grape molasses (pekmez)
- 1/2 cup sesame seeds

Instructions:

Activate the yeast:
- In a small bowl, combine the active dry yeast, sugar, and lukewarm water. Stir gently and let it sit for about 5-10 minutes, or until the mixture becomes frothy.

Prepare the dough:
- In a large mixing bowl, combine the all-purpose flour and salt. Make a well in the center and pour in the activated yeast mixture and olive oil.
- Use a wooden spoon or your hands to mix everything together until a dough forms.
- Transfer the dough to a floured surface and knead for about 8-10 minutes, or until the dough is smooth and elastic.

Let the dough rise:
- Place the dough in a lightly greased bowl, cover it with a clean kitchen towel or plastic wrap, and let it rise in a warm, draft-free place for about 1-2 hours, or until doubled in size.

Shape the simit:

- After the dough has risen, punch it down to release the air. Divide the dough into 10 equal portions.
- Roll each portion of dough into a long rope, about 20-22 inches (50-55 cm) long. Twist the ends together to form a circle and pinch the ends to seal.

Prepare the molasses mixture:
- In a shallow bowl, mix together the molasses and 2 tablespoons of water.

Coat with sesame seeds:
- Dip each shaped simit into the molasses mixture, making sure to coat it evenly.
- Then roll the coated simit in sesame seeds, pressing gently to adhere the seeds to the dough.

Bake the simit:
- Preheat your oven to 400°F (200°C). Place the sesame-coated simit on a baking sheet lined with parchment paper.
- Bake in the preheated oven for about 15-20 minutes, or until the simit is golden brown and cooked through.

Serve:
- Once baked, remove the simit from the oven and let them cool slightly before serving.
- Enjoy your homemade Turkish-style simit bread warm or at room temperature, as a delicious snack or alongside your favorite dips and spreads.

These freshly baked simit breads are perfect for breakfast, brunch, or as a tasty snack any time of the day. Enjoy their chewy texture and nutty sesame flavor!

Moroccan-style spiced olives

Ingredients:

- 2 cups olives (such as green or black, brine-cured or oil-cured)
- 2 cloves garlic, sliced
- 1 tablespoon olive oil
- 1 teaspoon ground cumin
- 1 teaspoon ground coriander
- 1/2 teaspoon paprika
- 1/4 teaspoon ground cinnamon
- Pinch of cayenne pepper (optional, for heat)
- 1 lemon, thinly sliced (optional)
- Fresh herbs (such as parsley, cilantro, or thyme) for garnish

Instructions:

Prepare the olives:
- If using olives packed in brine, rinse them under cold water to remove excess salt. If using olives packed in oil, you can skip this step.
- Place the olives in a bowl or jar large enough to accommodate them.

Add the flavorings:
- Add the sliced garlic, olive oil, ground cumin, ground coriander, paprika, ground cinnamon, and cayenne pepper (if using) to the olives.
- Toss the olives until they are evenly coated with the spices and garlic.

Optional: Add lemon slices
- If desired, add thinly sliced lemon slices to the olives. The acidity of the lemon adds brightness to the dish.

Marinate the olives:
- Cover the bowl or jar with a lid or plastic wrap and let the olives marinate in the refrigerator for at least 4 hours, or preferably overnight. This allows the flavors to meld together.

Serve:

- Before serving, let the olives come to room temperature. Garnish with fresh herbs, if desired.
- Moroccan-style spiced olives can be served as part of a mezze platter, alongside cheese and charcuterie, or as a snack on their own.
- Leftover olives can be stored in an airtight container in the refrigerator for up to a week.

Enjoy these Moroccan-style spiced olives with their aromatic blend of spices and garlic, perfect for adding a burst of flavor to any meal or snack!

Egyptian-style ful medames

Ingredients:

- 2 cups cooked fava beans (canned or dried)
- 2 cloves garlic, minced
- 1/4 cup fresh lemon juice
- 2 tablespoons olive oil
- 1 teaspoon ground cumin
- Salt, to taste
- Optional toppings: chopped fresh parsley, diced tomatoes, diced onions, hard-boiled eggs, tahini sauce, pickled vegetables, chili flakes

Instructions:

Prepare the fava beans:
- If using dried fava beans, soak them in water overnight. Drain and rinse the soaked beans.
- Cook the soaked or canned fava beans in a pot of boiling water until they are tender, about 1-2 hours for dried beans or 10-15 minutes for canned beans. Drain the cooked beans and set them aside.

Mash the fava beans:
- In a large bowl, mash the cooked fava beans using a fork or potato masher until they reach your desired consistency. Some people prefer a smoother texture, while others like to keep it chunky.

Season the ful medames:
- Add the minced garlic, fresh lemon juice, olive oil, ground cumin, and salt to the mashed fava beans. Mix well to combine and adjust the seasoning to taste.

Serve:
- Transfer the seasoned ful medames to a serving dish.
- Serve the ful medames warm or at room temperature, drizzled with extra olive oil and topped with your choice of optional toppings such as chopped fresh parsley, diced tomatoes, diced onions, hard-boiled eggs, tahini sauce, pickled vegetables, or chili flakes.

- Enjoy the ful medames with flatbread, pita bread, or crusty bread for dipping.

Ful medames is a nutritious and satisfying dish that's packed with protein, fiber, and flavor. It's a versatile dish that can be customized with various toppings and enjoyed for breakfast, brunch, lunch, or as a snack any time of day.

Armenian-style cheese burek

Ingredients:

For the dough:

- 1 package of phyllo pastry sheets, thawed if frozen
- 1/2 cup unsalted butter, melted

For the cheese filling:

- 2 cups crumbled feta cheese
- 1 cup shredded mozzarella cheese
- 1 cup ricotta cheese
- 1/4 cup chopped fresh parsley
- 1/4 cup chopped fresh dill (optional)
- 1 egg, beaten
- Salt and pepper to taste

Instructions:

Prepare the cheese filling:
- In a mixing bowl, combine the crumbled feta cheese, shredded mozzarella cheese, ricotta cheese, chopped fresh parsley, chopped fresh dill (if using), beaten egg, salt, and pepper. Mix until well combined. Set aside.

Assemble the burek:
- Preheat your oven to 375°F (190°C). Grease a baking dish with butter or oil.
- Place one sheet of phyllo pastry on a clean work surface. Brush it lightly with melted butter. Place another sheet of phyllo pastry on top and brush it with butter as well. Repeat this process with 4-5 sheets of phyllo pastry, stacking them on top of each other.
- Spread a layer of the cheese filling evenly over the stacked phyllo pastry sheets, leaving a border around the edges.
- Roll up the phyllo pastry sheets tightly into a log, starting from one short end. Place the rolled burek seam side down in the prepared baking dish.

- Repeat the process with the remaining phyllo pastry sheets and cheese filling to make additional burek rolls.

Bake the burek:
- Brush the tops of the burek rolls with melted butter.
- Bake in the preheated oven for 25-30 minutes, or until the burek is golden brown and crispy on top.

Serve:
- Once baked, remove the Armenian-style cheese burek from the oven and let them cool slightly before serving.
- Slice the burek into individual portions and serve warm as a delicious appetizer, side dish, or snack.

This Armenian-style cheese burek is a delightful pastry filled with a creamy and flavorful cheese mixture. Enjoy its crispy layers and savory filling!

Turkish-style spinach and feta omelette

Ingredients:

- 3 large eggs
- 1 tablespoon milk or water
- Salt and pepper, to taste
- 1 tablespoon olive oil or butter
- 1 cup fresh spinach leaves, chopped
- 1/4 cup crumbled feta cheese
- Optional: chopped tomatoes, onions, bell peppers, or herbs for additional flavor

Instructions:

Prepare the eggs:
- Crack the eggs into a mixing bowl. Add the milk or water, salt, and pepper.
- Whisk the eggs vigorously until well combined and frothy. Set aside.

Cook the spinach:
- Heat the olive oil or butter in a non-stick skillet over medium heat.
- Add the chopped spinach to the skillet and sauté for 2-3 minutes, or until wilted. Season with a pinch of salt and pepper.
- If using any additional vegetables such as tomatoes, onions, or bell peppers, you can add them to the skillet and sauté until softened.

Add the eggs:
- Pour the whisked eggs evenly over the sautéed spinach and vegetables in the skillet.
- Let the eggs cook undisturbed for a minute or two, allowing the bottom to set.

Add the feta cheese:
- Sprinkle the crumbled feta cheese evenly over one half of the omelette.

Fold and finish cooking:
- Using a spatula, carefully fold the other half of the omelette over the side with the feta cheese, creating a half-moon shape.
- Let the omelette cook for another 1-2 minutes, or until the eggs are fully cooked and the cheese is melted.

Serve:
- Slide the Turkish-style spinach and feta omelette onto a plate.
- Garnish with fresh herbs or additional feta cheese if desired.
- Serve the omelette hot, accompanied by toast, bread, or a side salad.

This Turkish-style spinach and feta omelette is a delicious and satisfying meal that's packed with protein and flavor. Enjoy it for breakfast, brunch, or any time of the day!

Moroccan-style honey and almond pastries (M'hanncha)

Ingredients:

For the almond filling:

- 2 cups almonds, blanched and finely ground
- 1/2 cup granulated sugar
- 1 teaspoon ground cinnamon
- 1/4 teaspoon ground cardamom
- Zest of 1 lemon
- 1 tablespoon orange blossom water (optional)
- 1/4 cup melted butter or ghee

For the pastry:

- 1 package phyllo pastry sheets, thawed if frozen
- 1/2 cup melted butter or ghee

For garnish:

- Honey, for drizzling
- Sliced almonds, for decoration
- Powdered sugar, for dusting (optional)

Instructions:

   Prepare the almond filling:
   - In a mixing bowl, combine the finely ground almonds, granulated sugar, ground cinnamon, ground cardamom, lemon zest, and orange blossom water (if using). Mix until well combined.
   - Gradually add the melted butter or ghee to the almond mixture, stirring until it forms a thick paste. Set aside.

   Assemble the pastry:
   - Preheat your oven to 350°F (175°C). Grease a baking sheet or line it with parchment paper.

- Lay one sheet of phyllo pastry on a clean work surface and brush it lightly with melted butter or ghee. Place another sheet of phyllo pastry on top and brush it with butter as well. Repeat this process with 5-6 sheets of phyllo pastry, stacking them on top of each other.
- Spread a thin layer of the almond filling evenly over the stacked phyllo pastry sheets, leaving a border around the edges.
- Roll up the phyllo pastry sheets tightly into a log, starting from one short end. Repeat this process with the remaining phyllo pastry sheets and almond filling to make additional rolls.

Shape the pastry:
- Coil each log of filled phyllo pastry into a spiral shape, resembling a snake or coil. Place the coiled pastries on the prepared baking sheet.

Bake the pastries:
- Brush the tops of the coiled pastries with melted butter or ghee.
- Bake in the preheated oven for 25-30 minutes, or until the pastries are golden brown and crispy.

Serve:
- Once baked, remove the Moroccan-style honey and almond pastries from the oven and let them cool slightly.
- Drizzle the pastries generously with honey and sprinkle sliced almonds over the top.
- Optionally, dust the pastries with powdered sugar for an extra touch of sweetness.
- Serve the pastries warm or at room temperature, sliced into portions.

These Moroccan-style honey and almond pastries are a delightful combination of crispy phyllo pastry and fragrant almond filling, perfect for serving as a dessert or sweet treat on any occasion. Enjoy their delicious flavor and beautiful presentation!

Turkish-style fried eggplant with yogurt and garlic (Ali Nazik)

Ingredients:

For the eggplant:

- 2 medium-sized eggplants
- Salt
- Olive oil for frying

For the yogurt sauce:

- 1 cup Greek yogurt
- 2 cloves garlic, minced
- Salt to taste

For garnish:

- 1 tablespoon butter
- 1 teaspoon paprika (optional)
- Chopped fresh parsley or mint leaves

Instructions:

Prepare the eggplant:
- Peel the eggplants and slice them lengthwise into 1/2-inch thick slices.
- Sprinkle salt over the eggplant slices and let them sit for about 15-20 minutes. This helps to draw out excess moisture and bitterness from the eggplant.
- After 15-20 minutes, rinse the eggplant slices under cold water and pat them dry with paper towels.

Fry the eggplant:
- Heat some olive oil in a large skillet over medium-high heat.
- Working in batches, fry the eggplant slices until golden brown and tender, about 3-4 minutes per side. Add more oil as needed.
- Once fried, transfer the eggplant slices to a plate lined with paper towels to drain any excess oil.

Prepare the yogurt sauce:
- In a mixing bowl, combine the Greek yogurt, minced garlic, and salt to taste. Mix well until smooth and creamy.

Assemble the dish:

- Arrange the fried eggplant slices on a serving platter.
- Spoon the yogurt sauce over the eggplant slices, spreading it evenly.
- In a small saucepan, melt the butter over low heat. Stir in the paprika, if using, and cook for a minute or two until fragrant.
- Drizzle the melted butter mixture over the yogurt sauce.
- Garnish with chopped fresh parsley or mint leaves.

Serve:

- Serve the Turkish-style fried eggplant with yogurt and garlic (Ali Nazik) immediately, while still warm.
- Enjoy it as a delicious appetizer or side dish, accompanied by bread or rice if desired.

This dish offers a wonderful combination of flavors and textures, with the creamy yogurt sauce complementing the crispy fried eggplant. It's a popular and satisfying dish in Turkish cuisine.

Armenian-style tahini cake

Ingredients:

- 1 cup tahini (sesame paste)
- 1 cup granulated sugar
- 3 large eggs
- 1 teaspoon vanilla extract
- 1/2 cup milk
- 1 1/2 cups all-purpose flour
- 2 teaspoons baking powder
- 1/4 teaspoon salt
- Optional: 1/2 cup chopped walnuts or sesame seeds for garnish

Instructions:

Preheat the oven: Preheat your oven to 350°F (175°C). Grease and flour a 9-inch round cake pan or line it with parchment paper.

Mix the wet ingredients: In a mixing bowl, combine the tahini, granulated sugar, eggs, and vanilla extract. Beat together until well combined and smooth.

Add the dry ingredients: In a separate bowl, sift together the all-purpose flour, baking powder, and salt. Gradually add the dry ingredients to the wet ingredients, alternating with the milk, and mixing until just combined. Be careful not to overmix.

Bake the cake: Pour the batter into the prepared cake pan and spread it out evenly. Optionally, sprinkle chopped walnuts or sesame seeds on top for garnish.

Bake in the preheated oven: Bake for 30-35 minutes, or until a toothpick inserted into the center comes out clean and the top is golden brown.

Cool and serve: Remove the cake from the oven and let it cool in the pan for about 10 minutes. Then, transfer it to a wire rack to cool completely.

Slice and serve: Once cooled, slice the Armenian-style tahini cake into wedges and serve. You can enjoy it plain or with a dusting of powdered sugar, a dollop of whipped cream, or a drizzle of honey, depending on your preference.

This Armenian-style tahini cake is wonderfully moist and has a subtle nutty flavor from the tahini. It makes for a delightful dessert or snack, perfect for enjoying with a cup of tea or coffee.